Holiday
PHOTO

Tricks

100 Spot-the-Difference Puzzles

· Photographs by Robin Fox

STERLING INNOVATION
An imprint of Sterling Publishing Co., Inc.

New York / London
www.sterlingpublishing.com

STERLING, the Sterling Logo, STERLING INNOVATION, and the Sterling Innovation logo are registered trademarks of Sterling Publishing Co., Inc.

2 4 6 8 10 9 7 5 3 1

Published by Sterling Publishing Co., Inc.
387 Park Avenue South, New York, NY 10016

Distributed in Canada by Sterling Publishing
c/o Canadian Manda Group, 165 Dufferin Street
Toronto, Ontario, Canada M6K 3H6
Distributed in the United Kingdom by GMC Distribution Services
Castle Place, 166 High Street, Lewes, East Sussex, England BN7 1XU
Distributed in Australia by Capricorn Link (Australia) Pty. Ltd.
P.O. Box 704, Windsor, NSW 2756, Australia

Printed in China

Sterling ISBN 978-1-4027-5981-9

For information about custom editions, special sales, premium and corporate purchases, please contact Sterling Special Sales Department at 800-805-5489 or specialsales@sterlingpublishing.com.

Table of Contents

Introduction

Do you have a sharp eye? The pairs of holiday themed pictures in this book may appear to be exactly the same—but they're not! Do you notice anything different? Is something missing? Is there something that wasn't there before? Look closely and see if you can "Spot the Differences" in these fabulous photos showing some of your favorite holiday scenes!

Puzzles are categorized into three levels of difficulty: Bright, Dazzling, and Brilliant. There are five differences to "spot" in bright, six in dazzling, and seven in brilliant. Answers appear at the back of the book.

Good Luck!

BRIGHT

● ● ● ● ● ● ● ● ● ● ● ●

Answer on page 126

Answer on page 126

Answer on page 127

Answer on page 127

Answer on page 128

Answer on page 128

Answer on page 129

Answer on page 129

Answer on page 130

Answer on page 130

Answer on page 131

Answer on page 131

Answer on page 132

Answer on page 132

Answer on page 133

Answer on page 133

Answer on page 134

Answer on page 134

Answer on page 135

Answer on page 135

Answer on page 136

Answer on page 136

Answer on page 137

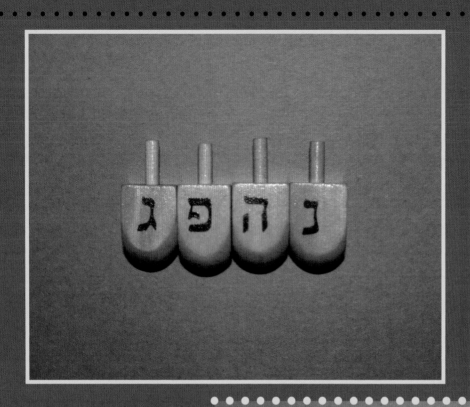

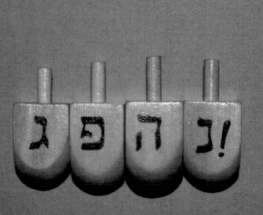

Answer on page 137

Answer on page 138

Answer on page 138

Answer on page 139

Answer on page 139

Answer on page 140

Answer on page 140

Answer on page 141

42

Answer on page 141

43

Answer on page 142

DAZZLING

Answer on page 142

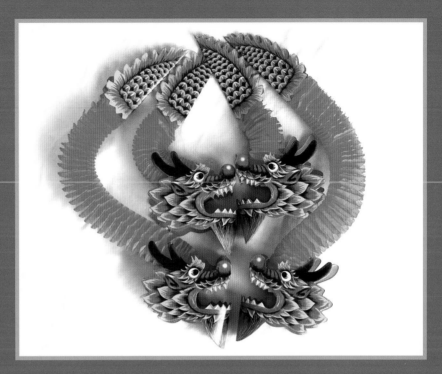

Answer on page 143

Answer on page 143

Answer on page 144

Answer on page 144

Answer on page 145

Answer on page 145

Answer on page 146

Answer on page 146

Answer on page 147

Answer on page 147

Answer on page 148

Answer on page 148

Answer on page 149

Answer on page 149

Answer on page 150

Answer on page 150

You will be unusually successful in business.

You will solve all these really fun picture puzzles.

Answer on page 151

Answer on page 151

Answer on page 152

Answer on page 152

Answer on page 153

Answer on page 153

Answer on page 154

Answer on page 154

Answer on page 155

Answer on page 155

Answer on page 156

Answer on page 156

Answer on page 157

Answer on page 157

Answer on page 158

Answer on page 158

Answer on page 159

BRILLIANT

● ● ● ● ● ○ ○ ○ ○ ○ ○ ○ ○

Answer on page 159

Answer on page 160

Answer on page 160

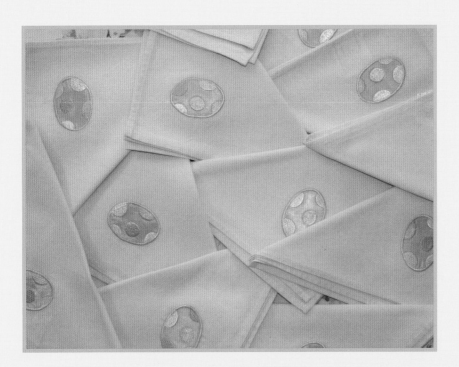

Answer on page 161

Answer on page 161

Answer on page 162

Answer on page 162

Answer on page 163

Answer on page 163

Answer on page 164

Answer on page 164

Answer on page 165

Answer on page 165

Answer on page 166

Answer on page 166

Answer on page 167

Answer on page 167

Answer on page 168

Answer on page 168

Answer on page 169

Answer on page 169

Answer on page 170

Answer on page 170

Answer on page 171

Answer on page 171

Answer on page 172

Answer on page 172

Answer on page 173

"OOOmph! Get your arm out of my mouth!"

Answer on page 173

Answer on page 174

Answer on page 174

Answer on page 175

Answer on page 175

ANSWERS

Puzzle page 6

Puzzle page 7

Puzzle page 8

Puzzle page 9

Puzzle pages 10-11

Puzzle pages 12-13

Puzzle page 14

Puzzle page 15

Puzzle pages 16-17

Puzzle page 18

Puzzle page 19

Puzzle page 20

Puzzle page 21

Puzzle page 22

Puzzle page 23

Puzzle page 24

Puzzle page 25

Puzzle pages 26-27

Puzzle page 28

Puzzle page 29

Puzzle page 30

Puzzle page 31

Puzzle pages 32-33

Puzzle page 34

Puzzle page 35

Puzzle page 36

Puzzle page 37

Puzzle pages 38-39

Puzzle page 40

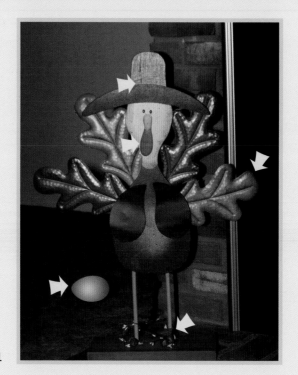

Puzzle page 41

Puzzle page 42

Puzzle page 43

Puzzle page 44

Puzzle page 46

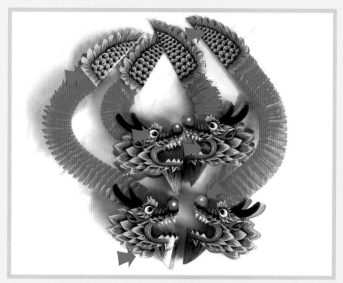

Puzzle page 47

Puzzle page 48

Puzzle page 49

Puzzle pages 50-51

Puzzle page 52

Puzzle page 53

Puzzle page 54

Puzzle page 55

Puzzle pages 56-57

Puzzle page 58

Puzzle page 59

Puzzle pages 60-61

148

Puzzle page 62

Puzzle page 63

Puzzle pages 64-65

Puzzle page 66

You will solve all these really fun picture puzzles.

Puzzle page 67

Puzzle page 68

Puzzle page 69

Puzzle pages 70-71

Puzzle page 72

Puzzle page 73

Puzzle page 74

Puzzle page 75

154

Puzzle page 76

Puzzle page 77

Puzzle pages 78-79

Puzzle page 80

Puzzle page 81

Puzzle page 82

Puzzle page 83

Puzzle pages 84-85

Puzzle page 86

Puzzle page 88

Puzzle page 89

Puzzle page 90

Puzzle page 91

Puzzle pages 92-93

Puzzle page 94

Puzzle page 95

Puzzle page 96

Puzzle page 97

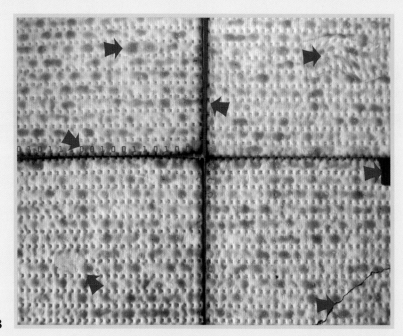

Puzzle page 98

Puzzle page 99

Puzzle pages 100-101

Puzzle page 102

Puzzle page 103

Puzzle page 104

Puzzle page 105

Puzzle page 106

Puzzle page 107

Puzzle pages 108-109

Puzzle page 110

Puzzle page 111

Puzzle page 112

Puzzle page 113

Puzzle page 114

Puzzle page 115

Puzzle pages 116-117

Puzzle page 118

Puzzle page 119

Puzzle page 120

173

Puzzle page 121

Puzzle page 122

Puzzle page 123

Puzzle page 124